W9-BFH-411

CENTER

Also Written by George Sullivan
and Illustrated by Don Madden

Pitcher
Quarterback
Run, Run Fast!

CENTER

George Sullivan

illustrated with photographs

and with line drawings by
Don Madden

Thomas Y. Crowell   New York

Center

Library of Congress Cataloging-in-Publication Data
Sullivan, George, 1927–
  Center.

  Summary: Explains the technical skills and strategies
it takes to be a center in basketball.
    1. Basketball—Coaching—Juvenile literature.
2. Centers (Basketball)—Juvenile literature.
[1. Centers (Basketball) 2. Basketball] I. Madden, Don,
1927–   ill. II. Title.
GV885.3.S85   1988   796.32′32   85-48245
ISBN 0-690-04580-8
ISBN 0-690-04582-4 (lib. bdg.)

ACKNOWLEDGMENTS

Many people helped in the preparation of this book. The author is especially grateful to coaches Frank Caeser and Kevin Boyle of Xavier High School in New York City and their players. Special thanks are also due Francesca Kurti, T.L.C. Custom Labs; Aime LaMontagne; and Tim Sullivan.

Contents

1 What It Takes   3
Conditioning   6
The Right Attitude   6

2 Passing   9
The Chest Pass   10
The Bounce Pass   11
The Overhead Pass   12
The Baseball Pass   13
Receiving Passes   14

3 Shooting   15
The Jump Shot   16
The Lay-up   20
Stuffing   22
The Hook Shot   23
Second Shots   25

4   Jump Balls   27

5   Free Throws   29

6   Rebounding   35
Jumping Up   36
Defensive Rebounding   38
Offensive Rebounding   40

7   On Offense   43
Driving for the Basket   45
The Give-and-Go   45
The Pick-and-Roll   46
Setting Screens   47
Analyzing the Opposition   47
Foul Trouble   47

8   Playing Defense   51
Defensive Stance   52
Shot Blocking   55
"Reading" Your Opponent   55

9   Winning and Losing   57

1
What It Takes

A professional basketball player was once asked about the importance of the center. "Why do you think they call the position 'center'?" he answered. "Because he's always in the middle of things."

It's true—in basketball, everything revolves around the center.

The two guards should excel in defense and setting up plays. The two forwards are chiefly scorers and rebounders.

The center has to have all-around talents. He or

she has to be a good scorer, skilled with the one-hand jump shot. The center has to be able to help hold down the opposition scoring by blocking shots.

The center also has to be quick and deft as a ball handler, able to pass to forwards driving for the basket or guards whenever they get open.

Rebounding is another skill the center must have. He or she has to be willing and able to leap up and grab the ball as it comes caroming off the backboard or rim.

Shooter. Passer. Playmaker. Shot blocker. Rebounder. These are the jobs the center must be able to do. No player is more important to the team.

Conditioning

The center is usually the tallest player on the team. But being tall for your age isn't enough. You also have to be in first-class physical condition.

When your team gets possession of the ball, you, as the center, must race down the court to help set up the scoring play. Then, when the opposition takes over the ball, you have to hurry back to the other end of the court to play defense. You're practically a nonstop player.

Extra jogging or running will help you to build your stamina.

You may also want to try some push-ups or chin-ups to increase your upper body strength. More muscle power will help you to be a better rebounder.

You may want to consider a weight-training program, too. But don't lift weights without the supervision of a coach or trainer.

The Right Attitude

You may have the ability to lead your team in scoring, but that doesn't mean you should shoot whenever you have a chance. A high-scoring player doesn't necessarily make a basketball team a winning team. It takes five players working together.

It takes teamwork.

As the center, you should always try to draw upon the individual skills of your teammates. You should know how each can contribute.

Who is the best ball handler? Who has the most accurate outside shot?

Try to make each player a star. That's teamwork. That's what it takes to win.

2

Passing

Anytime your team gets possession of the ball, your strategy should be to get the ball to the open player closest to the basket. Passing is the way to do this.

Be certain of your passes. Never release the ball unless you're sure the pass is going to be completed.

Be sure to have a target when you pass. Usually you'll want to hit the receiver about chest high. That makes it easy for the receiver to grab the ball and instantly shoot or dribble.

The speed of the pass must always be right for the situation. It doesn't do any good to whip the ball hard to a teammate who is only five feet away from you.

There are several different types of passes. You should know how to deliver each one.

The Chest Pass

This is the simplest pass to throw. Use it anytime there's a clear path between you and the receiver.

Hold the ball at about chest level, gripping it on both sides. To release, step in the direction of the

pass. Snap your wrists. Your thumbs turn down; your wrists turn out.

The Bounce Pass

The bounce pass is a special kind of chest pass. Use it when the ordinary chest pass is likely to be blocked. Your target is a spot on the floor between you and the receiver.

Be careful about using the bounce pass. Since it travels at a low level and its speed is slowed by the bounce, it can be easily intercepted. You probably won't use it more than once or twice in a game.

The Overhead Pass

Since most of your passes will be delivered in heavy traffic, this is the pass you'll use more often than any other. Raise the ball high above your head. Grasp it on the sides; the tips of your thumbs should be pointing toward one another.

As you release the ball, step in the direction of the pass. Snap your wrists hard. Your palms should end up facing the floor.

The Baseball Pass

This is the pass to use when you want to fire the ball a long distance in a hurry. You're likely to use it after grabbing a rebound, targeting a teammate who is sprinting down the court.

In executing the pass, first bring the ball back behind one shoulder, then whip your throwing arm forward, snapping your wrist as you release.

At the same time, shift your weight from the rear foot to the front foot. This weight shift puts power and distance into the throw.

Receiving Passes

Whenever you're on the court, be ready to receive a pass. When the ball is tossed your way, relax. Your hands should give a little when the ball arrives.

Protect the ball by holding it at about waist level and close to your body. If you're tightly guarded, raise it over your head while you decide whether to shoot or pass.

Don't think in terms of dribbling—that is, advancing the ball by bouncing it. Centers seldom dribble. Since they're taller than average, the ball takes high bounces and is difficult to protect.

3
Shooting

Shooting is the first skill young players develop. Most feel that it is more important than any other—and it is.

As a center, you should practice shooting all the time. But don't overlook the other skills the position demands. Work on your passing and rebounding, and on playing defense, as much as your shooting.

The Jump Shot

It doesn't matter where you play the game—in a garage driveway, a local playground or the school gym—your most important shot is the jump shot.

When you shoot a jumper, the idea is to release the ball at the very peak of the jump. This puts the ball at a point higher than the defender can reach. In other words, the jump shot gives you a clear shot at the basket.

Your body should be solidly balanced before you attempt the shot. Your feet should be about shoulder width apart.

If you shoot with your right hand, your right foot should be slightly closer to the basket than your left foot. Your shoulders should be square to your target.

Bend at the knees. The power for the shot comes from the arm and wrist, the feet and legs—but mostly from the legs. The farther you are from the basket, the deeper you should bend.

As you're bending your knees, get the ball set. Spread the fingers of your shooting hand, supporting the ball from behind. There should be a little bit of space between your palm and the sur-

face of the ball. Use your other hand to help control the ball.

The elbow of your shooting arm points toward the basket. Notice how the forearm and hand can now pump forward and back, with the elbow acting as a hinge.

Before you put the ball up, take aim. Most players target on the middle of the back of the rim. Remember, you're not going to shoot at the basket, but *into* it.

Leap straight up. As your legs straighten, snap your shooting wrist forward. Release the ball off your fingertips.

Follow through. After you've released the ball, your hand should continue on a path toward the rim. This puts the right spin on the ball, helping it fall into the basket.

When you're a good distance from the basket, arch your shot so it soars above the level of the rim. This increases the chance it will go in.

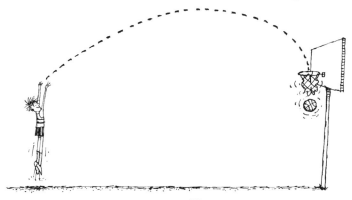

The Lay-up

The lay-up is the shot to use whenever your path to the basket is clear. It often comes at the end of a fast break, or following a steal or scramble for the ball.

Drive toward the basket, building up as much speed as you can without losing control of the ball.

As you get close, push off your inside foot, the foot that is closest to the basket. As you go up, bend the knee of your outside leg up toward the basket.

Pick out your target. It should be a spot on the backboard about a foot higher than the rim, and on the side of the backboard from which you're approaching. Concentrate on your target until you see the ball hit it.

Hold the ball in both hands, and start shifting it to your shooting hand as you go up. The back of your hand should be facing your forehead as you push the ball toward the target.

Practice lay-ups until you can make just about every one. There's nothing worse than missing an easy lay-up.

You should eventually become skilled at laying up the ball with either hand from both sides of the basket. In other words, you should be able to make four kinds of lay-ups:

With the right hand from the left side.
With the right hand from the right side.
With the left hand from the left side.
With the left hand from the right side.

Aime LaMontagne

Stuffing

You can be a very effective center without once stuffing the ball. But every young player feels the urge to leap up and jam the ball down into the net from above, at least once in a while. Stuffing—also called dunking—can electrify the fans and give your team an emotional boost.

Of course, you have to be taller than average to

be able to stuff. (The hoop, after all, is ten feet above the floor.) Most coaches say a prospective stuffer should stand at least an inch or two above six feet.

Try stuffing with a tennis ball first. Work up to a volleyball, then go to a basketball.

Be careful. There's always a chance you can slam your hand or wrist against the rim. Injured fingers or even a broken bone can be the result.

The Hook Shot

The hook is another basic weapon for the center. Since it's almost impossible to defend against, the hook can be extremely effective.

Aime LaMontagne

The hook is used from close range. You begin with your back to the basket. The ball is in both hands.

Suppose you're shooting with your right hand. Start turning to your left, pivoting on your left foot. Your head turns too. Focus on your target, a spot on the backboard above the rim.

As you're turning, sweep your right arm toward the basket. The arm should almost brush your right ear as it sweeps by.

Release the ball when your hand is at the highest point of its arc. Snap your wrist forward. Let the ball roll off your fingertips.

Be sure to follow through. You end up facing the basket, your right arm in front of your body.

Second Shots

Every time you shoot, follow the ball to the basket. If the shot misses, go up for the rebound. Once you have the ball in your grasp, go right back up with it.

4
Jump Balls

A jump ball is the method used to put the ball in play at the beginning of a game. Two opposing players face each other in the center circle across the mid-court line. The referee tosses the ball up between them. Each leaps and tries to tap the ball to a teammate.

As its center and probably its tallest player, you'll represent your team in such jump-ball situations.

When you're lining up for a jump, stand sideways to the mid-court line. Your feet should be comfortably apart. Bend at the knees. Keep most of your weight on your rear foot.

Watch the referee as he gets set to toss the ball up. Concentrate on his hands.

When the ball goes up, shift your weight forward and leap straight up off your front foot. Swing your arm up, tapping the ball at the highest point of your leap.

Most teams have one or more plays to be used in jump-ball situations. Usually the play calls for the center to tap the ball back; that is, toward the basket the team is defending. The center targets one of the guards. Other times the center tries to tap the ball to one of the forwards, who breaks for the opposition basket.

It isn't easy to tap the ball in the right direction.

5

Free Throws

The free throw is the shot you're awarded when you're fouled by an opponent. It's called a "free" throw because no one is permitted to guard you as you shoot.

You shoot from the free-throw line, which is 15 feet from the basket. You have 10 seconds in which to get your shot off.

A free throw is worth one point. When the foul is committed against a player who is shooting at the basket, the penalty is two free throws. This gives the player a chance to get the two points the basket would have been worth.

Free throws are very important. Indeed, most close games are decided by free throws.

As the team's center, and always in the thick of things, you're likely to draw more fouls and thus be awarded more free throws than any of your teammates. That's one reason you should work hard to become a good free-throw shooter.

The secret to success from the free-throw line is doing the same thing every time. Establish a routine, then stick to it.

Decide what type of shot you're going to use. Most players rely on a one-hand jump shot, but they don't actually jump into the air. They merely rise up on their toes as they release the ball.

Get your feet set in a comfortable position behind the line. If you're a right-handed shooter, you'll want to have your right foot slightly ahead of your left.

Relax. Take two or three deep breaths. Bounce the ball a couple of times.

Pick out your target on the back of the rim. Imagine the arc the ball is going to take traveling from your fingertips to the target.

31

Get the ball set in your shooting hand. Bend your knees.

Then fire. Straighten your legs, pump your arm and snap your wrist. Rise up on your toes as you send the ball on its way.

When you practice free throws, practice seriously. Imagine that each one you take can win a pro or college championship for your team.

Shoot thirty free throws every day. Keep a record of how many you make. Try to improve from one month to the next. By the time you get to high school, you should be making six to seven free throws out of every ten you attempt.

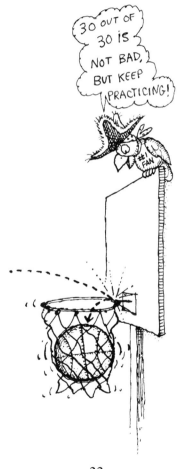

6
Rebounding

Get to the backboard and grab that rebound! Statistics show that the team that controls the boards wins.

It's easy to understand why. When the shooting team gets the rebound, it means another chance to shoot. When the defensive team gets the rebound, it kills the opposition's scoring threat.

A quick and determined rebounder can dominate a game. But rebounding is no cinch. Every opposition player wants the ball. There's plenty of shoving and bumping. You're going to feel some knees and elbows. But you can't let that bother you. Pretend it's *your* ball; it's got your name on it. Go and get it!

Jumping Up

Anytime you're getting set to go up for a rebound, start from a low stance. Your knees should be bent, your weight on the balls of your feet.

Explode off your toes, timing yourself so that you reach the ball at the highest part of your leap.

Pull the ball to your body to protect it. Let your elbows stick out.

Naturally, the higher you leap, the more rebounds you're going to grab. Jumping rope is a good way to improve your jumping ability. Jump with both feet first, then the right foot, then the

left. Keep trying to increase the number of jumps you can do in a given amount of time—in five minutes, say, or ten.

Defensive Rebounding

Suppose the opposition has just brought the ball across the mid-court line. Before a shot is taken, get in a defensive position between the player you're covering and the basket.

Then, when the shot goes up, box out your opponent. (This is also called blocking out.) If you can keep the player boxed out, the rebound is going to drop in front of you.

Once the shot is in the air, anticipate the direc-

tion the rebound is going to take. Is it going to carom to the right? To the left? Straight back? Or where?

Turn and face the basket. Back into the player you're guarding. Shove your backside into the player's thighs. Stick your elbows out, and keep one hand in contact with the player so you can follow his or her moves.

As soon as you see the ball is within reach, go for it. You should be picking out a teammate to pass to as you come down with the ball. Get the pass off as fast as you can.

This pass is called an outlet pass. Often it goes to a guard and is used to trigger a headlong drive toward the opposition basket—a fast break. The idea is to score before the opposition can get set up on defense.

Offensive Rebounding

When one of your teammates takes a shot and misses, get to the basket as quickly as you can. Leap up, grab the ball and then go right back up with it.

Sometimes your opponent may block you out, and you won't be able to get both hands on the ball. Using one hand, try tipping the ball up to the basket. Or try tapping it to one of your team-mates.

You really don't have to grip the ball at the offensive end of the court. The important thing is to keep it alive for another shot.

Aime LaMontagne

7
On Offense

Every coach has his or her idea of what kind of offensive system is best. But no matter what type of offense your coach installs, it is a good bet that you as the center will be playing the post.

This means that you'll be stationed with your back to the basket much of the time, passing off to your teammates and, in general, serving as the core of your team's offense. It is also called playing the pivot.

If you're taller than the average center and a good rebounder, you'll probably play a low post position; that is, close to the basket.

If you are about average height for a center and able to move well, and have a good outside shot, you may play a high post. This means that you'll be positioned at about the free-throw line, and move from one side to the other.

The high post offense puts an emphasis on quickness. Move decisively. Snap those passes.

Whether you play a high post or low post, your success depends on your ability to get open. If your guards and forwards can't get the ball to you, your team is going to be powerless.

Getting open may be difficult if you're tightly guarded. Your instinct is to run away from the player defending you. But doing the opposite works better. Run into the defender, make contact; then stop and dart away. It's not likely the defensive

player will be able to stay with you.

Another tactic is to run a tight circle around the player defending you. Signal for a pass when you work free.

Driving for the Basket

Once you're set in the pivot and the ball arrives in your hands, you have several choices. You can simply spin and shoot, you can hand off to a teammate driving for the basket, or you can drive for the basket yourself.

Drive when you think you can beat the player defending you. As you drive, push the ball out in front of you, bouncing it once. Keep your head up.

When you get close to the basket, grasp the ball in both hands and go up for the shot.

If your defender has a hard time covering you when you drive to the right, keep driving to the right until the defender learns to correct his or her mistake. Then fake to the right and drive left.

The Give-and-Go

A teammate passes the ball to you and breaks for the basket, and you shoot that teammate a return pass. This is called the give-and-go.

The Pick-and-Roll

When you set a pick for a teammate, you position your body so that it is in the way of his or her defender. The defensive player is unable to follow your teammate. The teammate is then free to get in position to receive a pass or to shoot.

To set a pick, run up to your teammate's defender. Get your chest in front of the player's shoulder. Spread your feet wide apart. Keep your hands at your sides.

Your teammate can then run right past you for the basket. As soon as you see your teammate is free, "roll" to the basket yourself. Get ready to go up for the rebound.

Setting Screens

A screen is similar to a pick, except that it always results in a shot being taken. Position yourself in front of an opposition player in order to prevent that player from keeping up with your teammate. Then, while the opponent tries to get around you, your teammate can take a shot, or receive a pass and then shoot.

Analyzing the Opposition

In the opening minutes of a game, study the opposition. Take advantage of whatever weaknesses the defense reveals.

Suppose the defensive players close in on you whenever you set up in the pivot. This is sure to mean one or more of your teammates is going to be open for a pass. Fire the ball to an open player.

Or instead, the defense may concentrate on covering your guards and forwards. That's when you should start shooting more.

Foul Trouble

When you're playing the pivot—that is, when you're setting up plays and driving for the basket—you're going to be making contact with opposition play-

ers. That means you'll occasionally cause a foul.

Fouls are called for such illegal acts as pushing, charging, holding and elbowing.

The fouled player's team may be awarded possession of the ball. At other times, the fouled player is awarded one or more free throws. If you should accumulate five personal fouls, you're sent to the bench for the remainder of the game. (In professional basketball, it takes six fouls to get suspended.)

There are some things you can do to help avoid fouls. Once they've gotten possession of the ball in the pivot, most centers try to keep opposing players away by turning their shoulders and elbows, first in one direction, then in the other. Never swing your elbows only. That's illegal.

Or suppose you're guarding a player who likes to dribble the ball. You think you can knock the ball loose. Go for it with an upward slap. When you swing your hand downward, you're more likely to hit the dribbler's hand or arm—and a whistle results.

Don't feel badly when you commit a foul because you were playing all out. In fact, if you never foul, that could be a bad sign. It could indicate that you're not playing as hard as you should be.

8
Playing Defense

Years ago, the center was supposed to be a scoring machine, stuffing points like crazy. That's changed. While the center is still counted upon to score well, he or she is also expected to hold down the opposition scoring.

The basic rule of defense states that you must keep your body positioned between your opponent and the basket. But this isn't always easy. It takes an extra measure of desire to play good defense. You have to push yourself.

Defensive Stance

Keep alert on defense, your body ready to move in any direction. Your feet should be about shoulder width apart, one foot slightly ahead of the other. Your weight should be evenly distributed.

Keep your back straight. Keep your chin up. Bend your knees, not your waist.

When you want to move to one side or the other, use a gliding step. Suppose you want to move to the right. Slide the right foot to the right, then slide the left foot.

What you don't want to do is cross one foot in front of the other. That puts you off balance.

When your opponent gets the ball, put on extra pressure. Move in close, get your hands up, wave them frantically. Get set to block his or her move. Don't relax for a second.

Shot Blocking

It's not easy to block an opponent's shot. It takes balance, timing and the ability to jump at least as high as the shooter.

It also takes knowledge of the shooter's form and style. Study your opponent. Notice how he or she gets the ball into a position to shoot. Get to know the rhythm of the opponent's shot.

When you leap to make your attempt to block, go straight up, not into the shooter. Flick at the ball with your fingers; don't slap at it. Be careful not to knock it out of bounds.

"Reading" Your Opponent

Try to pick out your opponent's strengths and weaknesses, and act accordingly.

If your opponent is skilled with the jump shot, move in very close. Play a jump shooter almost shirt-to-shirt.

Don't let an opponent get set in a favorite shooting spot. When the two of you come down the court, beat the player to that spot.

If your opponent is a clever dribbler, determine which is his or her favorite dribbling hand. If it's the right hand, force the player to switch to the left hand.

Of course, your responsibilities on defense go beyond the player you happen to be guarding. You should also be alert, ready to help out your teammates.

Suppose a rival player with the ball slips by one of your teammates and starts heading for the basket. Switch off the player you're guarding and cut off the opponent's path to the basket.

9
Winning and Losing

Everyone wants to be a winner. But nobody wins all the time.

There are going to be days when you're unable to keep your opponent from scoring, days the hoop seems to have a lid on it every time you put the ball up.

Don't be afraid of losing. It's all right to lose— as long as you do your best.

When your team does lose, congratulate the winners. Tell them, "Nice game." Then go back to the gym, practice harder and try to beat them next time.